Submarines

by Michael Green

Content Consultant:
Jack A. Green, Historian
Naval Historical Center

CAPSTONE PRESS

MANKATO, MINNESOTA

C A P S T O N E P R E S S
818 North Willow Street • Mankato, Minnesota 56001
http://www.capstone-press.com

Printed in the United States of America.

Library of Congress Cataloging-in-Publication Data
Green, Michael, 1952-
    Submarines/by Michael Green.
    p. cm. -- (Land and sea)
    Includes bibliographical references and index.
    Summary: Introduces the development, uses, possible weaponry, dangers, and locomotion of submarines.
    ISBN 1-56065-555-0
    1. Submarines (Ships)--United States--Juvenile literature.
[1. Submarines.] I. Title. II. Series: Land and sea (Mankato, Minn.)

V858.G74 1998
623.8'257--dc21

                    97-5908
                      CIP

                        AC

Editorial credits
Editor, Timothy Larson; Cover design, Timothy Halldin; Illustrations, James Franklin; Photo Research Assistant, Michelle L. Norstad
Photo/Illustration credits
Michael Green, 8
Unisys Corporation/Jan-Willem Boer, 34
U.S. Coast Guard, 38
U.S. Naval Institute Collections, 41
U.S. Navy, cover, 4, 6, 11, 12, 15, 20, 23, 26, 28, 30, 33, 36, 47

Table of Contents

Chapter 1

Submarines

Military submarines are warships. They can run on the surface of the water and underwater. A warship is a ship with guns or other weapons that navies use for war. Sub is a shortened word for submarine.

A submarine is submerged when it dives below the surface of the water. Throughout history, navies have tried to build submarines that are both fast and able to submerge deep underwater.

Submerged submarines are difficult to spot from the surface. This feature allows subs to move close to enemy ships and attack them. It also allows subs to patrol areas unseen.

Many navies call submarines, boats. Sailors nicknamed early subs, pig boats. This was because the air inside the subs was stale and it stank.

Military submarines are warships. They can run on the surface of the water and underwater.

Many submarines have cigar-shaped hulls.

The U.S. Navy has built and commissioned many different types of submarines. A commission is a navy order to put a ship into service. The navy has named its subs after sea creatures, cities, and important people.

The U.S. Navy puts subs that are alike into groups called classes. Each class has special features like their forms or kinds of engines. The navy names each class after the first ship in the group. The navy creates a new class for each new type of sub it commissions.

Submarine Form

Many submarines have long, cigar-shaped hulls. A hull is the body of a submarine. Most military subs have two hulls. One hull fits inside the other. The hulls help protect a sub and its crew from enemy explosives. The hulls also keep a sub from being crushed by water pressure during deep dives. Water pressure is the weight of water that presses on submerged objects.

Submarine hulls are streamlined. Streamlined means shaped to travel easily through water. The long, rounded hulls of many submarines are streamlined shapes. Navies sometimes change the shape of submarine hulls to improve streamlining.

Submarines have hatches built into them. A hatch is a door that seals tightly to keep out water. Many hatches on a sub are for entering and leaving a sub. Some hatches are for escaping a sub.

Military submarines do not have windows. On the surface, sailors can open hatches to look outside. Underwater, sailors use periscopes and

A conning tower is centered on the top of most military submarines.

sonar to see where they are going. A periscope is a long tube with mirrors. It helps sailors look above the surface of the water. Sonar is machinery that uses sound waves to measure depth and to locate objects underwater.

Conning Tower

An enclosed tower is centered on the top of most submarines. This tower is the conning tower. Some sailors call the conning tower the fin or the sail.

A conning tower has two vents. A vent is an opening or pipe through which air enters and smoke or fumes escape. One vent is called the snort induction mast. This vent pulls in air for a sub's engines. The other vent is called the exhaust. It pulls engine fumes out of a sub.

The conning tower also contains a submarine's periscopes and radar antennas. Radar is machinery that uses radio waves to locate and guide things. An antenna is a wire that sends out and receives radio waves. Radar antennas work when a sub is on the surface. They are housed inside the conning tower when a sub is underwater.

Inside a Military Submarine

Many military submarines have two decks inside of them. The decks are divided into sections called compartments. Sailors live and work in these compartments.

The control room is the most important compartment on a military submarine. The control room contains all the instruments the captain and sailors use to control a sub. Sailors also look through a sub's periscopes there.

A military sub also has compartments for sleeping. Some compartments are for cooking and eating. Some house a sub's engines. Others are for storing and launching torpedoes. A torpedo is an explosive that travels underwater. Launch means to set into action.

Many submarines have special compartments such as airlock chambers. An airlock chamber seals out water from the rest of the sub. It helps divers leave a submerged sub without flooding the sub. Some subs have large compartments to store and launch missiles. A missile is a special explosive that flies long distances.

Submerging a Submarine

Sailors add ballast to make a submarine submerge. They reduce ballast to make a sub rise to the surface. Ballast is weight such as water. Ballast

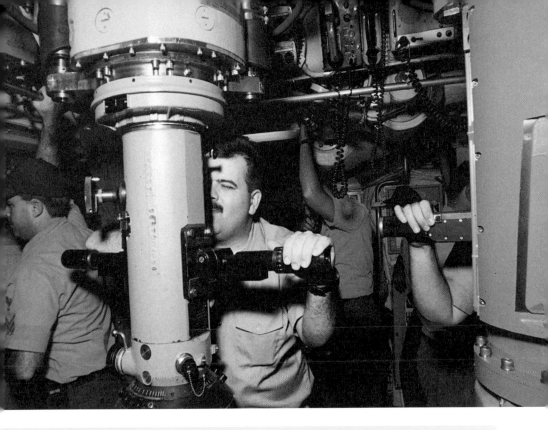

Sailors look through a submarine's periscopes in the control room.

tanks hold a sub's ballast. Military submarines use seawater for ballast.

To submerge a submarine, sailors open valves on the ballast tanks. A valve is an opening that can be opened or closed. The open valves allow seawater to pour into the tanks.

Many military submarines have had fuel-powered engines like this one.

Sailors also open other valves on the ballast tanks to let out air. As the tanks fill, the ballast increases and the submarine sinks. The sailors then close all the valves.

To make a submarine rise, sailors open the valves. The seawater is pumped out of the ballast tanks. Air fills the tanks and the sub rises. Today, navy subs can reach and return from depths of

more than 2,300 feet (750 meters). Depth
means deepness.

Steering

Diving planes help sailors steer a submarine. A
diving plane is a metal plate that tilts a sub up and
down. Diving planes are located at the bow and the
stern of a sub. The bow is the front of a sub. The
stern is the rear of a sub. On some subs, diving
planes are on the conning tower, too.

A submarine also has rudders. A rudder is a
metal plate. It steers a sub right and left in the
water. A submarine's rudder is located at the stern.
Propellers called screws are also located at the
stern. Screws turn and push subs through water.

Engines, Speed, and Distance

Many military submarines have fuel-powered
engines and battery-powered electric motors. On
the surface, a fuel-powered engine provides the
power to turn a sub's screws. Underwater, the
electric motor turns a sub's screws. The electric
motor's batteries charge as a sub travels on
the surface.

Some modern submarines have nuclear-powered engines. Nuclear power is a special kind of energy. It lasts longer than other kinds of energy. Nuclear fuel comes in the form of rods. Rods are nuclear-charged metal bars.

People measure the speed of ships and submarines in knots. One knot is 1.15 miles per hour. The fastest navy subs have had top speeds of 50 knots. This is about 58 miles (74 kilometers) per hour.

In the past, submarines moved more slowly underwater than on the surface. By the 1950s, better streamlining and engine designs made it possible for subs to travel distances more quickly underwater.

Submarine Weapons

A submarine's most important weapons used to be its torpedoes. Torpedoes are used to attack enemy ships and subs. Sailors fire torpedoes from torpedo tubes built into a sub's bow and stern. Today, subs still carry improved kinds of torpedoes.

Submarines also had antiaircraft guns on their conning towers. Antiaircraft guns are guns

Today's U.S. Navy submarines carry torpedoes like this one.

designed to shoot planes. Subs also had large deck guns mounted on their top decks. These guns were used to shoot small enemy ships.

Since the late 1950s, guided missiles have been the most important weapons on subs. A guided missile is a missile that is guided to its target by radar. Today, some of these missiles have ranges up to 8,000 miles (12,800 kilometers).

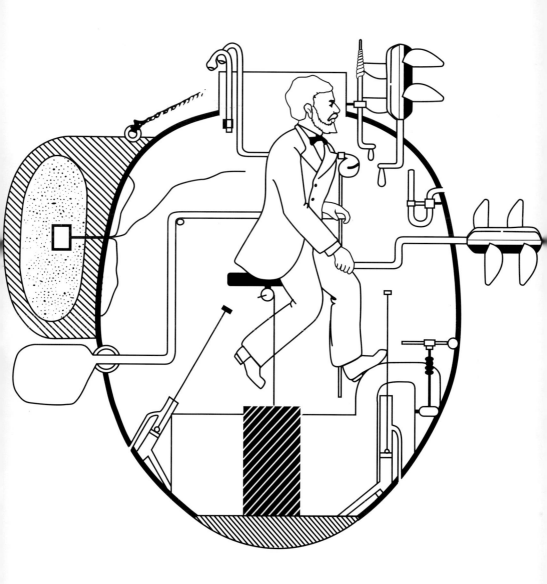

Chapter 2

Early Submarine History

The first submarine was made by Cornelius Drebbel in 1620. His sub was a 12-person rowboat covered with oilskin. Oilskin is leather soaked in oil to make it waterproof. Sailors rowed the sub to make it move. Drebbel's sub could not move very fast or dive very deep.

In 1775, inventor David Bushnell built the first military submarine. He named his sub the *Turtle*. The submarine was made of wood and was shaped like an egg. It had a few windows. It also had screws and a rudder. The *Turtle* could hold only one sailor and could not dive very

The *Turtle* was the first military submarine. It was shaped like an egg and could only hold one person.

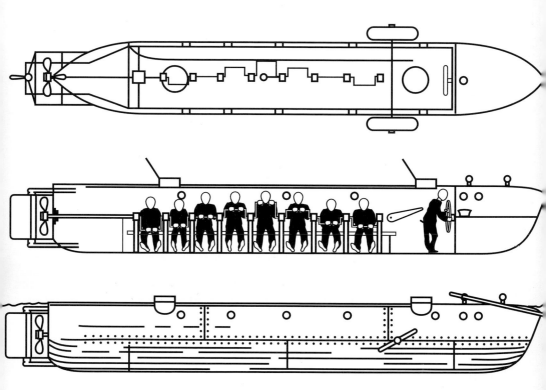

deep. The sailor had to power the *Turtle*'s screws by hand.

Bushnell made the submarine to help the colonists fight the British during the Revolutionary War (1775-1783). Colonists are people who settle distant lands but remain governed by their native country. The *Turtle* never sank a ship.

Better Submarines

The first time a submarine sank a ship was during the Civil War (1861-1865). The Civil War was the war between the Northern and Southern United States. The Northern states were called the Union. The Southern states were called the Confederacy. In 1864, a Confederate navy submarine named the *Hunley* sank a Union warship.

The *Hunley* was hand powered and armed with a large package of explosives. The explosives were mounted on the end of a long, wooden pole. The pole was located on the bow of the *Hunley*. Sailors steered the *Hunley* so the pole rammed the explosives into the Union warship.

The *Hunley* was the first submarine to sink a ship during wartime.

The *Holland* was the U.S. Navy's first gasoline-powered submarine.

Engine-powered Submarines

In 1898, inventor John Holland built the first submarine powered by gasoline engines and batteries. The new sub was named the *Holland* after its inventor.

A gasoline engine powered the *Holland* on the surface. Its batteries powered the sub underwater. The *Holland* carried a seven-sailor crew. Its top speed was five knots.

The U.S. Navy decided to buy the *Holland* in 1900. It was the navy's first submarine. But the sub's engine gave off fumes. The fumes stank and often poisoned the sub's crew. These fumes are why sailors nicknamed early gasoline-powered subs, pig boats.

Problems

The *Holland* and later gasoline-powered subs had other problems, too. On the surface, their engines needed fresh air to work. The engines also used a lot of fuel. Underwater, the subs' battery power did not last very long. These problems kept the subs from diving very deep or traveling very far.

In 1906, inventors created the diesel engine. A diesel engine uses fuel similar to gasoline. The new engine had advantages. The fumes from the diesel engine were less harmful. The diesel engine also used less fuel than gasoline engines.

But the early diesel engines had problems, too. Like gasoline engines, they also needed fresh air to work. The U.S. Navy did not have the money to replace the gasoline engines with diesel engines, either. Because of these problems, the navy did not use many diesel engines on subs until the 1930s.

World War I Submarines

During World War I (1914-1918), the German navy became the first navy to use a diesel-powered submarine in battle. In September 1914, a U-boat sank three British warships with torpedoes. German subs were called U-boats. The U stands for underwater.

The U.S. Navy did not use submarines very much during World War I. But the navy was impressed by how well German U-boats worked during the war.

Throughout the 1930s, the U.S. Navy built and tested many new submarines. All of the new subs had diesel engines and battery-powered electric motors.

World War II Submarines

U.S. Navy submarines helped fight battles with Japan during World War II (1939-1945). Much of Japan's ability to fight the war depended on its supply ships. Supply ships carried food, weapons, and ammunition. The Japanese could not fight as well without these supplies. Many U.S. Navy subs attacked Japanese supply ships.

The U.S. navy used 300 submarines during World War II. These submarines sank 1,178

U.S. Navy submarines sank 214 Japanese warships. This one can be seen through a U.S. Navy sub's periscope.

Japanese supply ships during the war. They also sank 214 Japanese warships. The Japanese destroyed 52 U.S. Navy subs.

The most common navy submarines in World War II were in the Gato/Balao class. Nineteen Gato/Balao class subs were destroyed during World War II.

The navy commissioned the first Gato/Balao class submarines in December 1941. The subs

World War II Naval Battles of the Pacific Ocean

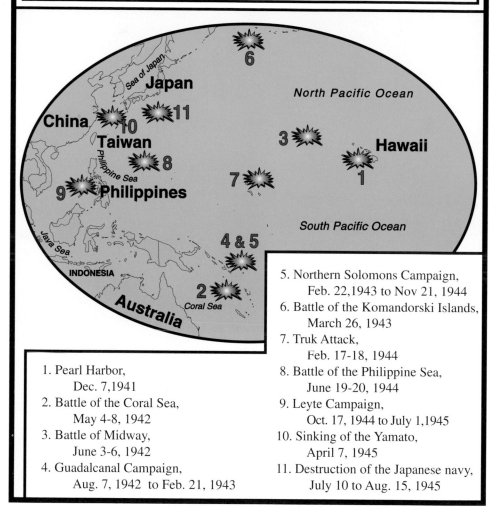

1. Pearl Harbor,
   Dec. 7, 1941
2. Battle of the Coral Sea,
   May 4-8, 1942
3. Battle of Midway,
   June 3-6, 1942
4. Guadalcanal Campaign,
   Aug. 7, 1942 to Feb. 21, 1943
5. Northern Solomons Campaign,
   Feb. 22, 1943 to Nov 21, 1944
6. Battle of the Komandorski Islands,
   March 26, 1943
7. Truk Attack,
   Feb. 17-18, 1944
8. Battle of the Philippine Sea,
   June 19-20, 1944
9. Leyte Campaign,
   Oct. 17, 1944 to July 1, 1945
10. Sinking of the Yamato,
    April 7, 1945
11. Destruction of the Japanese navy,
    July 10 to Aug. 15, 1945

were 312 feet (94 meters) long and 27 feet (eight meters) wide. They had diesel engines and electric motors. Gáto/Balao class subs could run at 20 knots on the surface and at nine knots underwater. They could travel 300 to 400 feet (90 to 120 meters) below the surface. These subs each carried a crew of 60 sailors.

The *Growler*

The *Growler* is one of the best known Gato/Balao class submarines. On February 7, 1943, the *Growler* was patrolling on the surface near the Truk Islands. These islands are in the Pacific Ocean. Sailors on the *Growler* spotted a Japanese gunboat. A gunboat is a small military boat armed with guns.

Japanese sailors on the gunboat also spotted the *Growler*. They moved their boat to ram the sub. The captain and crew of the *Growler* were unable to fire their torpedoes. But they were able to steer the sub to escape the gunboat's ramming attack.

The *Growler* then rammed the gunboat and tore a hole in it. As the gunboat slowly sank, its crew fired the boat's guns at the *Growler*. The captain of the *Growler* was hit. He ordered his crew to submerge the sub without him. The *Growler* and its crew escaped to safety because of this order.

Chapter 3

Recent Submarine History

After World War II, the U.S. Navy wanted new submarines. The navy sold many of its old subs to its allies. Allies are countries that work together. Then the navy started working on improving sub design.

The navy streamlined its remaining submarines by removing their deck guns and antiaircraft guns. This improved the subs' speed. But the subs' engines were still a problem. With these engines, subs still could not stay underwater very long. They also could not travel very far.

The U.S. Navy removed antiaircraft guns and deck guns from its submarines after World War II.

The *Skipjack* had an underwater speed of 50 knots.

Since 1954, the navy has put nuclear-powered engines in its submarines. These engines work when a sub is on the surface. They also work when a sub is submerged. They allow subs to dive to deeper depths and refuel less often.

Since 1955, nuclear-powered submarines have been able to dive as deep as 2,300 feet (750 meters). Many of today's subs can stay submerged for months. These subs only need refueling every 15 years.

The *Nautilus* and the *Skipjack*

In 1954, the U.S. Navy commissioned the *Nautilus*. It was the navy's first nuclear-powered submarine. The *Nautilus* was the first sub that could travel faster underwater than on the surface. The sub had a surface speed of 22 knots and a submerged speed of 23 knots. The *Nautilus* carried a crew of 105 sailors.

The navy wanted to create a streamlined hull that would increase the speed of its new submarines. In 1959, the navy commissioned the nuclear-powered *Skipjack* submarine.

The *Skipjack* had a streamlined, whale-shaped hull. It had an underwater speed of 50 knots. This made the *Skipjack* the world's fastest submarine. A crew of 93 sailors operated the *Skipjack*.

The *George Washington*

In 1959, the navy commissioned the *George Washington*. This sub was the first submarine that

the navy armed with Polaris guided missiles. The *George Washington* carried 16 Polaris missiles.

The *George Washington* launched its missiles while submerged. The missiles each had a range of 1,200 miles (1,920 kilometers). Later Polaris missiles each had a range of almost 2,500 miles (4,000 kilometers).

The *George Washington* was the first in a class of five nuclear-powered submarines. Each of the subs were 382 feet (115 meters) long and 33 feet (10 meters) wide. These subs had a surface speed

of 15 knots and a submerged speed of 40 knots.
Each sub carried crews of 120 sailors.

Bigger and Better

Since the 1960s, the navy has built new types of
missile-armed submarines. All of them have been
nuclear powered. Each new class of subs has
been bigger and more powerful than the last.
Sailors call these large subs, boomers.

The newest missile-carrying submarines are in
the Ohio class. The Ohio class subs are 560 feet
(168 meters) long and 42 feet (13 meters) wide.
These subs have a surface speed of 28 knots and
a submerged speed of 30 knots. A crew of 163
sailors runs each submarine.

The navy has 18 of these submarines. Each
sub carries 24 Trident missiles. These missiles
each have a range of more than 8,000 miles
(12,800 kilometers).

Attack Submarines

The navy uses another type of nuclear-powered
submarines. These subs are attack submarines.
The navy commissioned these subs for battle with
enemy submarines. To perform this job, the navy

arms attack subs with torpedoes and short-range missiles.

Most of the navy's attack submarines are in the Los Angeles class. There are more than 50 Los Angeles class attack subs in service. These subs are 360 feet (108 meters) long and 33 feet (10 meters) wide.

Los Angeles class submarines have a surface speed of 22 knots. They have a submerged speed of 33 knots. A crew of 141 sailors operates each Los Angeles class sub.

The navy's newest attack submarine is called the *Seawolf*. The *Seawolf* entered service in 1996. It cost the navy more than $2 billion to build this sub. The *Seawolf*'s top speed and diving abilities are military secrets. The sub carries a crew of 134 sailors.

The U.S. Navy arms its attack submarines with short-range missiles.

Military Submarine

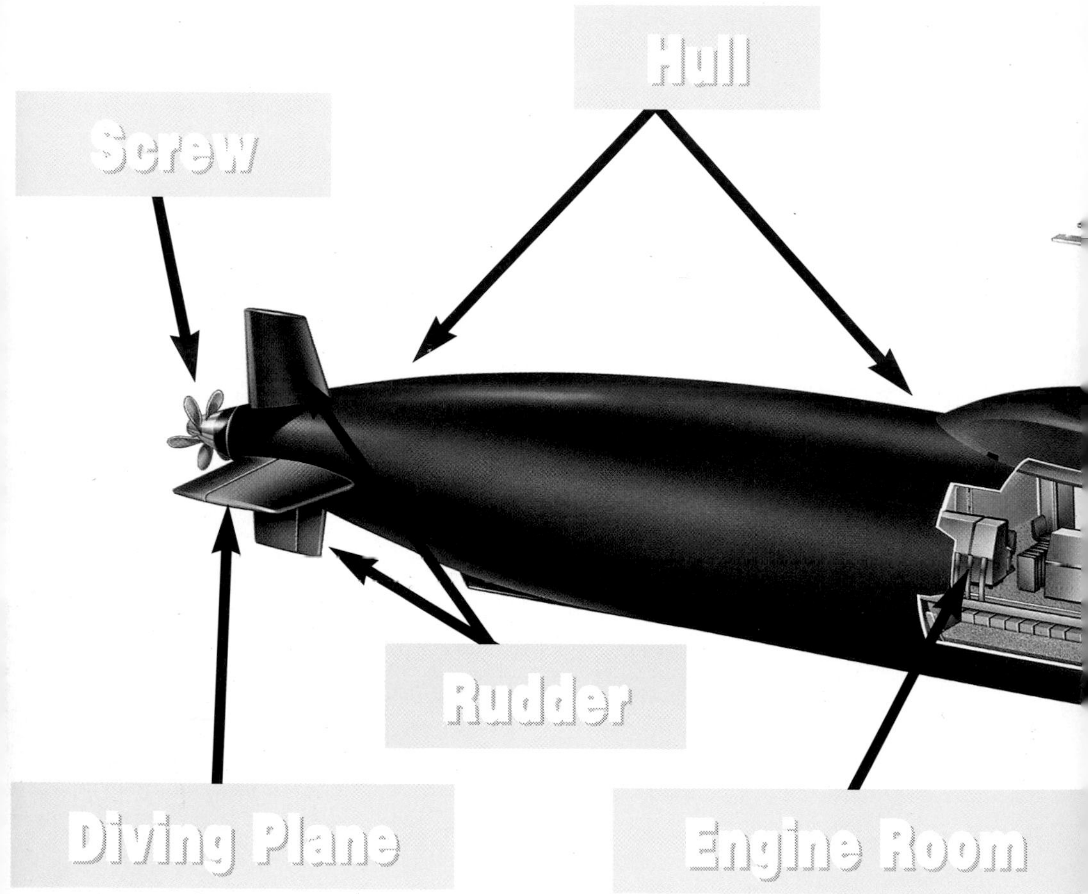

Hull

Screw

Rudder

Diving Plane

Engine Room

Illustration by Jan-Willem Boer
Copyright © 1989 Unisys Corporation

Conning Tower, Periscopes, Vents, and Antennas

Airlock Chamber and Hatch

Control Room

Hatches

Torpedo Tubes

Eating and Sleeping Compartments

Hull

Chapter 4

Safety and the Future

Traveling underwater is dangerous.
Accidents on a submarine can mean that the sub
never reaches the surface. Enemy explosives,
fires, engine failures, and leaks can be deadly for
sub crews.

The fuel that powers many of today's U.S.
Navy nuclear-powered submarines can be
dangerous, too. New and used nuclear rods are
harmful to people. Sailors must work carefully
with the rods. They also must store the rods in
safe containers. A container is a holder.

Because of these dangers, sailors are not
ordered to serve on subs. Instead, sailors

Sailors are not ordered to serve on U.S. Navy submarines.

volunteer to serve on navy submarines. Volunteer means to offer to do a job.

The navy teaches sub crews how to handle many of the dangers on submarines. Crews learn how to fight fires and repair damage. But sub crews also must depend on safety devices. Some devices help them escape sinking subs and rise safely to the surface. Others rescue sailors.

Safety Devices and Rescue

Submarine crews wear life jackets to escape a sunken sub. A life jacket is a jacket that helps people float in the water. Sailors use life jackets to rise to the water's surface. Life jackets can only be used at depths of less than 150 feet (45 meters). At greater depths, sailors run out of air before they can reach the surface.

Sailors used Momsen Lungs when they had to escape from greater depths. The Momsen Lung was created by U.S. Navy officer Charles B. Momsen in the 1930s. The Momsen Lung combined the life jacket and a breathing device.

Each Momsen Lung held 90 minutes worth of oxygen. In an emergency, sailors strapped Momsen Lungs on their chests. The devices lifted the sailors to the surface while giving them air to breathe.

A German sailor (middle) captured during World War II is shown wearing a Momsen Lung.

The U.S. Navy now uses two specially made, small submarines for sub rescues. They can reach sunken subs at many depths. Each small sub can carry 24 sailors to safety at one time. The subs are powered by small electric motors and have an underwater speed of four knots.

Future Submarines

The biggest threat to U.S. Navy submarines may be that they are no longer needed. The Soviet Union broke up in 1991. This ended tensions between that country and the United States. Today, many wars are much smaller than they used to be. A lot of navy subs simply are not needed.

The U.S. government is giving less money to the navy to build new submarines. Because of limited money, it is difficult for the navy to operate large numbers of subs.

Despite this trend, the navy still plans to build some more submarines. Many experts believe that the navy will return to diesel-powered subs in the future. They are smaller and cheaper to operate than nuclear-powered subs. What these next types of navy submarines will be is still a military secret.

The *Avalon* is shown attached to a larger submarine.

Words to Know

allies (AL-eyes)—countries that work together

antenna (an-TEN-uh)—a wire that sends out and receives radio waves

ballast (BAL-uhst)—weight such as water

colonists (KOL-uh-nists)—people who settle in distant lands but remain governed by their native country

commission (kuh-MISH-uhn)—a navy order to put a ship into service

conning tower (KAHN-ing TOU-ur)—a covered tower centered on the top of many submarine hulls

diesel engine (DEE-suhl EN-juhn)—an engine that uses fuel similar to gasoline

diving plane (DYV-ing PLANE)—a moveable metal plate on a submarine that tilts the sub up and down

guided missile (GIDE-ed MISS-uhl)—a missile that is guided to targets with radar

hatch (HACH)—a doorway that can be sealed tightly to keep out water

hull (HUHL)—the body of a ship or submarine

knot (NOT)—a measurement of speed for ships and submarines; 1.15 miles per hour

missile (MISS-uhl)—an explosive that flies long distances

nuclear power (NOO-klee-ur POU-ur)—a powerful kind of energy that lasts longer than other kinds of energy

oilskin (OIL-skin)—leather soaked in oil to make it waterproof

periscope (PER-uh-skope)—a long tube with mirrors that helps sailors view the surface from a submerged submarine

radar (RAY-dar)—machinery that uses radio waves to locate and guide things

rudder (RUHD-ur)—a moveable metal plate on a submarine that steers the sub right and left

sonar (SOH-nar)—machinery that uses sound waves to establish water depth and to locate objects

streamlined (STREAM-lined)—shaped to travel easily through water

torpedo (tor-PEE-doh)—an explosive that travels underwater

valve (VALV)—an opening that can be opened or closed

vent (VENT)—an opening or pipe through which air enters and smoke or fumes escape

To Learn More

Asimov, Isaac and Elizabeth Kaplan. *How Do Big Ships Float?* Milwaukee: Gareth Stevens, 1993.

Gibbons, Tony. *Submarines*. Minneapolis: Lerner Publications, 1987.

Graham, Ian. *Boats, Ships, Submarines and Other Floating Machines*. New York: Kingfisher Books, 1993.

Jordan, John. *Modern U.S. Navy*. New York: Salamander Books, 1986.

Lines, Cliff. *Looking at Submarines*. New York: Bookwright Press, 1984.

Useful Addresses

***Batfish* Submarine and Military Museum**
Box 253
Muskogee, OK 74401

Naval Historical Center
Washington Navy Yard
901 M Street SE
Washington, DC 20374-5060

The Submarine *Lionfish*
Battleship Cove
Fall River, MA 02721

Submarine Memorial Museum
P.O. Box 395
Hackensack, NJ 07602

Internet Sites

Naval Undersea Museum
http://www.tscnet.com/tour/museum/index.html

U.S.S. *Growler*
http://www.users.fast.net/~wa3key/growler.html

U.S. Navy History
http://www.history.navy.mil/

Navy: Welcome Aboard
http://www.navy.mil/

What the U.S. Navy's future submarines will look like is still a military secret.

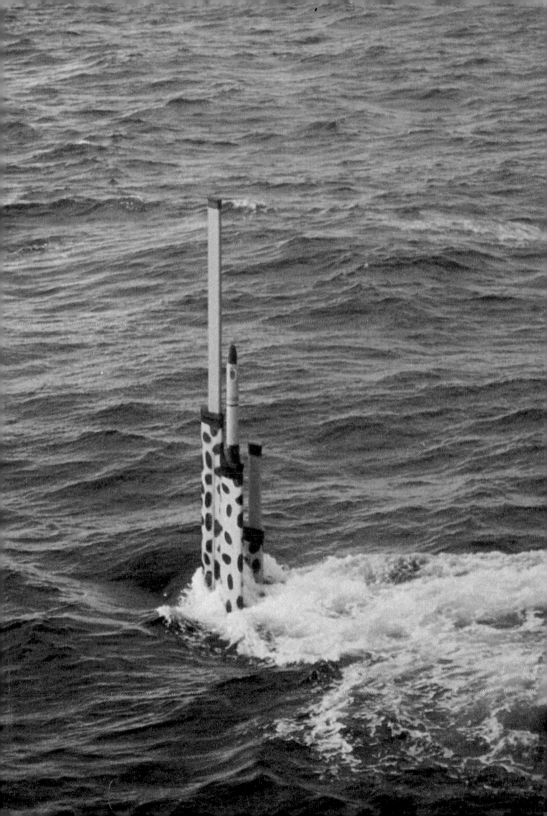

Index